Who Stole the Bases?

by Margo Sorenson

To Jim, Jane, and Jill, the best team in the world.
To Eric and Jason, who can make the big leagues.
To Jody and Sue, my major league editors.

M. S.

Cover Illustration: Greg Epkes
Inside Illustration: Michael A. Aspengren

11 12 13 14 15 16 17 18 19 20 PP 08 07 06 05 04

Contents

1

Where Are They?

"Hey!" Marty exclaimed. "Where are they? Where are the bases?" She peered into the shed. It was hard to see. The sun shining on the metal roof had blinded her.

Marty stepped inside. The shed was hot and dark. It smelled damp from last night's rain.

"Come on, Speedy!" Brett joked. "Hurry up! Let's make it *this* year, okay?"

The sun was hot on Marty's back. She squinted trying to see. Brett's cleats scuffed in the dirt as he walked up behind her.

"Cool your jets, hot shot! I'm doing the best I can. I just don't see them!" Marty said as she turned around. She made a face at Brett. He grinned back.

"What do you mean, you don't see them?" asked José, walking up. He pushed up next to Brett. He tried to look over Brett's shoulder into the shed.

"Let me see," added Dwight. He peered over everyone's shoulders. "Oh, great! No bases for practice."

Marty frowned. Her eyes scanned the inside of the shed. She could see the little machine that lined the baseball field. And there were the rakes. In one corner, some hoses were wound up like snakes. Team equipment bags lay in a heap.

Marty stepped farther inside. She moved the equipment bags. Nope, nothing there. She took one more look around just to be sure. There were no bases. What had happened to them?

Coach Espinoza jogged up. "Hurry up, kids, we have to practice. What's the problem?"

Marty backed out of the shed. She turned around to face the others.

"We can't find the bases, Coach!" Marty said. She shrugged her shoulders.

Coach Espinoza looked puzzled. "What?" he asked. He ducked his head and stepped into the dark shed.

Coach lifted up bags. He moved hoses aside. He came back out frowning.

"Well, you're right. They're not there," Coach said.

"Do you think maybe we left them out on the field after our last practice?" José asked.

"No," Coach Espinoza said. "We always take in our bases." He tipped back his baseball cap. He rubbed his forehead.

"Yeah," Brett agreed. "Dwight and I took them in last time. We're always tough on that." He elbowed Dwight. They grinned.

"They're right," Marty said. "I waited for them while they finished." Then she looked at Coach. "It was a *big* job for them. I thought I might have to help. But they finally did it!" she teased.

Coach Espinoza smiled. Then he looked puzzled. "And I know I locked the shed after practice," he said. "Maybe it was the team that practiced here yesterday. I wonder which team it was."

The rest of the Dodgers crowded around the shed. They muttered and talked to each other.

"It was probably those stupid Braves," said Ryan. "They're so dumb they forget which way is home plate!" A couple of kids laughed.

"Or," said Brett, his eyes gleaming, "maybe it wasn't the Braves. Maybe someone stole the bases."

Everyone stopped talking. Brett looked around at them.

"You know who I mean!" Brett said excitedly. "It could be that those losers, the Pirates, took the bases! I mean, think about it guys. Who are our worst enemies?"

Everyone began talking at once. The air filled with

chatter and laughter.

"Hey, José," Brett continued. "Remember when you caught that fly ball during our last game against the Pirates? Wasn't it Norris who yelled at you? Didn't he call you a loser? He said he'd get even. Remember?"

"And how about me?" Ryan added. He leaned down and rubbed his ankle. It had a brace on it. "How about when that jerk Randell slid right into me at third? His cleats were up. I know he did it on purpose, even though he said he didn't. Because of him, my ankle is wrecked. And a month without baseball pretty much wipes out the rest of the season."

The other Dodgers looked at Ryan's ankle. It still looked swollen even under the brace.

Brett looked at Marty. "Who's always putting our team down because we have a girl playing second base?"

Marty thought about all the cracks she had to put up with from the Pirates. "Yeah, yeah," she replied, "I'm used to it." She made a face.

"Oh, and how about when we line up to do high fives?" Marty continued. "Some of them spit on their hands first. Sick!"

"Then they rub their hands in the dirt too," added Dwight. He rubbed his hands on his pants.

Brett's eyes scanned the group. "Don't forget all the stuff they pull at school," Brett said. "How about the water balloon ambush by the gym?"

"Oh yeah!" Dwight said. He jammed his hat down on

his head.

"I remember that," José added. Then he smiled. " Course we got 'em back when we TP'd Bill's and Norris' houses right before it rained."

"Oooh, what a great mess that made!" remembered Marty.

Everyone smiled except Brett. "Well, this time the Pirates have gone too far," Brett said. "Stealing bases is pretty low, even for the Pirates. But they'll pay. I'll see to that."

"Just a second," Coach Espinoza broke in. "Let's not get carried away. We don't know what happened to the bases yet. I know you and the Pirates have a real rivalry going. But there could be other answers to this mystery. Think about it."

"Well," Marty offered slowly. "Maybe one of the other coaches borrowed them. Maybe he couldn't get them back in time for our practice. Or even some neighborhood kids could have taken them. Especially if another team was stupid enough to leave them out on the field," she said disgustedly.

"Yeah," Dwight said. "Or what about the park and rec people? They could have taken the bases to fix them or something."

"I was thinking that too," Coach Espinoza said. "I'll call the other coaches tonight. And the park and rec department. Somebody has to know where the bases are. And all of you, keep your eyes open. It could be some kids in the neighborhood, like Marty said." He motioned to the players. "Now let's play some baseball."

"But how can we practice without bases?" Ernesto asked.

"We'll just use gloves and some T-shirts for the bases," Coach answered. "It's not the best, but it'll work."

"Think you'll still be able to make those great tags at second?" teased Brett. Grinning, he pulled the bill of Marty's baseball cap down over her eyes.

"Hey, nobody gets under my tag," Marty replied. She pushed her cap back up. Her eyes shone with mischief. Then she stepped back on Brett's foot with her cleat.

"Ouch!" Brett yelled. He hopped up and down, holding his foot, pretending to be in pain.

"Oh, *sorry*," she teased.

"Okay, okay," Coach Espinoza said. "Quit fooling around. Let's warm up. And no more talk about the bases. Forget about the Pirates. Let's play ball."

The team formed two lines. They began throwing to each other.

Brett, Dwight, Marty, and José walked together to the ends of the lines.

"No way Coach is right. I know it was those losers, the Pirates," Brett said to José walking next to him. He thumped his glove with his fist.

"Yeah," José said. "They were pretty mad when they lost to us." He grinned for a minute. "Too bad for them!" he added.

"Yeah!" Brett agreed. "But I'd like to bust 'em right in their ugly faces. We can't let them pull stuff like this. Who knows what they'll try next? If they think they can get away with this..."

He stopped. He looked down at his catcher's mitt. "Next, they'll probably try to take our gloves." He narrowed his eyes.

José's face darkened. "They'd better not. This is the best glove I've ever had. I can't play without it. Remember when I forgot it at home last Saturday? Coach let me use his glove." José sighed. "But my whole game was off. I couldn't catch anything. I played lousy at shortstop!" He stared at his glove.

Dwight stared at his glove too. He squeezed it in his hand. It was brand new this season. He had worked hard for months to earn the money. "I finally got mine broken in," Dwight said. He rubbed a ball in the pocket.

"All I know is, I'm going to get the Pig-Heads—I mean, the Pirates," Brett said, turning to throw to José. He grinned. "This is war!"

"That's a good one," Marty giggled. "The War on the Pig-Heads! Good job, Brett!" She threw the ball to Dwight.

"I'll help you get 'em," said José. He threw the ball back to Brett. The sound of baseballs slapping into gloves echoed across the field.

Dwight jumped to snag a high toss. "You know what?" he called over to Brett. "I think you need to think over this Pirate thing. It might not be them. As Coach said, one of the other teams might know where the bases are." He threw the ball.

"Right. And Babe Ruth wasn't one of the greatest hitters in baseball," replied Brett. He grinned wickedly. "We're gonna get the Pirates good this time! Just wait!"

"Hey, come on," said Dwight. "Forget that. Let's just whip 'em on Saturday."

"Sorry," called Dwight when he overthrew the ball past Marty.

Marty turned around to chase the ball. It rolled toward the equipment shed. She looked past it at the street.

Something caught her eye. Her jaw dropped. No way, she thought.

Two guys on bicycles were turning the corner. She saw their faces just before they disappeared. Norris and Bill—Pirates! What were they doing hanging around?

Marty jogged back quickly. "Hey, guys. Come here!" she yelled.

Brett, José, and Dwight crowded around her. Dust rose in clouds from their cleats.

"I just saw Bill and Norris riding off," she said. "I think they took off when they saw me coming. What do you think they were doing?"

All four teammates turned around. They stared at the now-empty street beyond the fence that lined the park. Norris and Bill had disappeared.

"I can guess what they were doing," muttered Brett. "They were just checking out to see if we could practice without bases."

"Do you think so?" Dwight asked.

"Sure," Brett said. He tossed the baseball lightly. "Let's say you stole some bases so a team couldn't practice. Especially right before you were going to play them again. Wouldn't you like to ride by and see what they were doing?"

"Get going, you four," Coach Espinoza called.

Brett, José, Dwight, and Marty began throwing again. The balls thunked in their gloves.

Brett frowned and thought hard. Norris. What had Norris said to him at school yesterday? It had sounded weird to him then. But now, suddenly, it made sense.

"Hope you guys have a good practice tomorrow. *If* you can practice," Norris had said.

Brett reminded himself to tell José. José was the only one who seemed to understand what was going on. Dwight and Marty needed to wake up. They didn't think it was the Pirates. But he knew it was.

Dwight stretched his shoulder out. He looked at Brett's angry face. He was afraid Brett might lose his temper. He knew he'd have to stick close to Brett to make sure he didn't do something they'd all be sorry for.

Thunk! Dwight's throw landed in Marty's glove.

Marty thought about their rivalry with the Pirates. Stealing the bases sure seemed like something the Pirates might do. She just hoped things wouldn't get out of hand. She'd have to watch Brett and that temper of his.

2

The Twins Pitch In

"I'm home!" Brett yelled to his mom. He slammed the kitchen door. Then he tossed his bat bag on the kitchen floor.

"Yippee, skippee!" teased Shari. "Brett, we're sooooo glad you're home!" She jumped up and down, clapping her hands.

"Our favorite brother is home!" Shayna squealed. The twins danced around the kitchen table, pretending to be excited.

Brett groaned. How did he get so unlucky as to have twin sisters only a year and a half younger than he? And these days they were an even bigger problem. Bigger was right! Suddenly, they had grown so tall. He tried to avoid standing next to them. He *had* to grow some more—and soon.

Brett opened the refrigerator door. "I'm starved," he said. He looked around for something to grab.

"Ah-ah-ah," their mother said, walking into the kitchen. "You'll spoil dinner." She walked over to the refrigerator and closed the door gently in Brett's face.

"Aw, Mom," Brett complained. He headed over to the cupboard. Maybe he could grab a snack there. He glanced to see if Mom was watching him. Nope!

"I work hard all day. Then I come home and cook, even though I'm tired. I want you to eat your dinner," Mom said frowning. She opened the refrigerator again. She took out an onion and some ground beef.

Hah! Brett thought. He looked around at Mom again. She was unwrapping the ground beef. Quickly, he shoved a package of graham crackers into his pocket.

"Lighten up, Mom. Okay?" Brett said. "I'm just hungry after practice." He stuffed three graham crackers into his mouth.

"How was it today?" Mom asked. She began browning the meat in a pan.

"Fine—except—" Brett started to say. A big lump of graham cracker stuck in his mouth.

"Fine," Shayna broke in. "Except I struck out every time. And I couldn't make the throw to second base!" She and Shari giggled.

"You have an awfully fat mouth for a skinny fifth-grader," Brett snapped. He reached out and pulled Shayna's ponytail.

"Hey!" Shayna protested. She jerked her head away and patted her hair.

"Mom, don't let Brett talk to us like that," whined Shari.

The twins looked at each other slyly. Together, they turned down their mouths and tried to look sad.

"Girls," Mom sighed. "Girls, girls—and Brett too. Can we just call a truce for one night? I've had a tough day. How about a little peace and quiet?" She stopped chopping the onion. She looked at the three of them. "All right, Brett. What happened at practice?"

Brett swallowed the dry lump of graham crackers. "Someone stole our bases!" Brett exclaimed. "Right out of the shed! And I know who it was too—those losers, the Pirates!" He thumped his fist on the counter.

"Someone actually stole the bases?" Shari asked. Her eyes opened wide. She looked at Shayna.

"Right out of the shed?" Shayna added.

"Are you sure someone *stole* them?" Mom asked. "How do you know?" She broke up the ground beef with a spoon.

"I just know," Brett answered. "It had to be the

Pirates. They're always doing stuff to us."

Of course, they always got back at the Pirates. But Brett wasn't going to bring that up.

"They hate us," Brett continued. "Especially after we beat them last game." Brett's words tumbled out.

"But how do you *know* the bases were stolen?" Mom asked. The ground beef sizzled in the pan. She stirred it quickly. "Maybe someone borrowed them."

"Well, the bases are gone," Brett answered. "That's for sure. And the Pirates are always out to get us any way they can. The jerks. They almost busted Ryan's ankle in the last game. They're doing even more stuff to us at school."

Brett looked at his sisters. They were listening carefully. "They almost came right out and told us they were gonna do something to us at practice," Brett finished. He couldn't forget what Norris had said. He brushed the graham cracker crumbs off his hands.

"It sounds like a guess to me," Mom said slowly. "I can't believe Buddy Espinoza would accuse the Pirates of stealing your bases. Unless he had proof." She put the browned meat into a casserole dish.

"Well," Brett admitted, "Coach is checking out some other things. He said he'd call the other coaches and ask them about the bases. He's also going to call the rec center people.

"But as far as I'm concerned, he's wasting his breath," Brett said with confidence. "*I* know what happened.

"It has to be the Pirates," Brett continued. "You should

hear some of the stuff they've been doing and saying to us during games—and at school too. But we'll take care of those losers!" he threatened. "I'll see to that."

He paced around the small kitchen. He socked his fist into his open hand.

"Brett," Mom warned. "Watch your temper. You know what happens when you let your temper get out of control. And don't even think about doing anything at school."

She put the casserole in the oven. Just then the dryer buzzed. She sighed and hurried out of the room.

"So, what have the Pirates been saying at school?" Shayna asked. She gave Shari a long look.

"Well, for one thing, Randell told José we cheated. He said that's the only reason we beat them," Brett said angrily. He folded his arms and stared at the twins.

"Randell is one of the Pirates?" Shari asked. "Randell Jones?"

"Yeah, why?" Brett asked. What were the twins up to now?

"Oh—well—" Shari stopped and looked at Shayna. Shayna nodded her head.

"What?" Brett said impatiently.

"Well—there's a girl in my class—Heather Jones— and her brother's name is Randell," Shari said. "Her brother must be a Pirate." She paused.

"So what?" Brett snapped. Why did the Trouble Twins always take so long to get to the point?

"Well, we could call her up tonight. She might let something slip about the Pirates stealing the bases," Shayna said. A grin spread across her face. Her eyes sparkled with mischief.

"Then if you know the Pirates really did it..." Shari began. She looked at Shayna, smiling.

"You can *really* go after them!" Shayna finished, grinning. The girls gave each other a high five.

"I think you are all carrying this too far," Mom said, walking back into the kitchen. She put down a load of clothes and began to fold them. Then she looked at Brett.

"Brett, you watch yourself. Another fight at school and you'll get suspended." She snapped out a T-shirt and folded it.

Shari looked at Shayna. They grinned at each other.

"Girls, you watch yourselves too. Just stay out of this," Mom said. "You'll only make things worse." She smoothed out a pair of jeans.

Shari and Shayna looked at each other again. "Okay, Mom," they said together. They turned to go.

Mom glanced at the calendar tacked to the wall. "Brett, please wash your hands. It's your turn to set the table."

"Aw, Mom! I set it last night!" Brett complained. He slumped against the refrigerator.

"I don't think so!" Shari and Shayna said together. They had stopped in the doorway.

"Your brain is on overload worrying about those

19

stupid Pirates," Shari teased. She twirled her finger in the air next to her ear.

"If he *had* a brain, that is," Shayna snickered. She walked over to Brett. Quickly, she tapped the top of his head. "Oops! Hollow!" she said giggling.

"That's it, you little brat!" Brett yelped. He tried to grab Shayna's ponytail and missed.

"Missed! It's a miracle you catch *any* baseballs!" she called. She dashed out of the room with Shari right behind her.

"Mom, can't you control them?" Brett asked. He rubbed his head where Shayna had knocked it.

Mom smiled. "Not any more than I can control you," she said. "Now set the table, please. And forget about the Pirates and the bases and all that. You need to think about homework."

She rolled up some socks. Then she tucked them inside the basket of folded clothes.

"Homework," Brett repeated. "I—ah—don't have any homework," he fibbed. There was no way he was going to waste any time on homework tonight. He had more important things to do. Some plans to make. Revenge!

"Really?" Mom asked. She looked at Brett carefully. "Well, all right," she said shrugging her shoulders. "Do the table anyway. Your father will be home soon." She carried the basket of folded clothes out of the kitchen.

✳✳

After dinner, Shari and Shayna carried the plates to the sink. Mom and Dad went into the living room and turned on the TV.

"Now?" Shari whispered to Shayna. "Mom and Dad can't hear us." She smiled at Shayna. She scraped a plate into the sink.

"Yeah," Shayna replied. She grinned at Shari. Then she took the plate and rinsed it.

"Uh, Brett," Shari called. He was rifling through the cookie jar in the cupboard.

Brett had just popped a cookie into his mouth. "Uh-huh?" he said, through a mouthful of cookie.

"Eeeew," Shayna said. "Gross!"

"What do you want?" Brett said crossly. He sprayed some cookie crumbs. Then he opened his mouth. A gooey mass of cookie sat on his tongue. He knew they hated it when he did that. At least he could bug his sisters as much as they bugged him.

"*Sick*, Brett!" Shari exclaimed. Then she lowered her voice. "We talked to Randell's sister," Shari said in a whisper. She turned on the water hard. Shayna clattered the dishes.

Brett raised his eyebrows. "Oh, yeah?" he asked, interested. "And what did she say?" Then he narrowed his eyes. "You didn't tell her anything about stealing the bases, did you? You didn't tell her that we think the Pirates did it, did you?" He took a step toward them, frowning.

"No!" Shayna said quickly. She backed up against the sink.

"No way!" Shari echoed, squeezing up next to her.

"I don't want the Pirates to know we're planning anything," Brett warned. He folded his arms and leaned back against the counter.

"You can trust us," Shari said. She opened her eyes wide. She raised her eyebrows, trying to look innocent.

Yeah, right, Brett thought. He shook his head in disgust.

"Anyway," Shari went on, "she said that Randell was talking about your team two days ago. He said that your team would be really sorry you beat them last time. He laughed about something that was going to happen at practice. He said something about stealing bases!"

"What?" Brett yelled. He jerked forward. His hands doubled into fists.

"What's going on in there?" Dad complained from the living room. "We can't hear the TV!"

"Sorry, Dad," the twins said together.

Shari put her finger to her lips and looked at Brett. "Hold it down," she whispered.

They busily rinsed some dishes. Shayna ran the water hard. Dad turned back to the TV set.

"Those jerks!" Brett exploded. "Just wait till they find out what's coming to *them!*"

Bam! Bam! He thumped his fist on the counter.

"Brett, please!" Mom called.

"Okay, Mom," Brett said. He looked at Shari and Shayna. He frowned. "I'm gonna make some phone calls," he muttered.

Brett punched Dwight's number on the kitchen wall phone next to the back door. Then he stepped outside the house. He shut the phone cord in the back door. This was the only way he could talk on the phone without his nosy sisters hearing him.

"Good job!" Shayna giggled. She grinned at Shari.

"Teamwork," Shari added, giving her a high five. "We sure helped him out, didn't we?" Giggling, they turned back to the sink.

Outside, Brett waited impatiently for someone to answer.

"Hey," Brett said when he heard Dwight's voice. "We've got some work to do. I'm gonna punch out Randell tomorrow after school. Are you gonna come?"

"Why Randell?" Dwight asked. "What did he do now?"

"That jerk! He doesn't need to *do* anything. He should be punched out just for being himself. But I just found out something interesting," Brett said.

Thud! Thud! Brett kicked the side of the house with his shoe, over and over.

"My sisters just told me Randell was bragging to his little sister. He was talking about stealing our bases! I'm going on a cleanup detail. And his ugly face'll be the mop! I'm gonna rub his face into the sidewalk!"

Brett could feel his anger building. He couldn't wait to get ahold of Randell.

"Hey, man, calm down," Dwight said. "You can't be punching anybody out. You'll get suspended."

"Yeah, so what? Randell deserves it," Brett said loudly.

"Do you wanna play baseball or not? Your parents said they'd bench you for two games if you get into trouble at school," Dwight reminded him. "They'll do it too. You know that.

"And you're the best catcher on the team," Dwight continued. "I always pitch better when you're behind the plate. I need you. The team needs you."

"Yeah, yeah," Brett said. "So, we're just going to sit around and let those guys do whatever they want. I don't think so! I'm not letting anybody walk all over me!

"After school tomorrow, Randell's gonna pay," Brett said. "Here's my plan. Listen up."

3

A Plan for the Pig-Heads

"No, man, I don't want to hear it!" Dwight said into the phone. "For once, could you just keep yourself out of trouble?"

"Hey, buddy, don't you be telling me what to do," Brett argued. "If I want to punch him out, it's my business." He twisted the phone cord around and around his fingers.

"And then what am I gonna do for a catcher?" Dwight asked. "You know you'll be suspended."

"Are you going to be there or not?" Brett asked. He began to pace back and forth outside the back door. The phone cord stretched out its coils.

"No," Dwight said slowly. "I guess I would be there if I could. But my mother works tomorrow. I have to baby-sit my little brother." He sighed. "The story of my life."

"Yeah. Okay," Brett said. "But don't worry. I won't get suspended. You'll see." He began winding up the phone cord.

"I hope not," Dwight said. "Gotta go. Homework, you know."

"See ya," Brett said. He stepped inside and hung up the phone. Dwight's homework reminded him of what he should be doing. Good thing his parents weren't anywhere around to hear Dwight. Then they'd want to know why *he* wasn't doing *his* homework.

Brett frowned. So what if he got in trouble every now and then for not doing his homework. Nobody was perfect, right? Besides, who cared about verbs and all that stuff. Nobody was going to ask him what a verb was when he was 25 years old.

He dialed José's number. He took the phone outside again and closed the door behind him.

"Sure," José agreed after Brett told him what he was planning. "Sure, man. I'll be there for you."

Brett came back inside and hung up the phone. He grinned. Just wait until tomorrow. Then he remembered Marty. She was okay—for a girl. Plus, she was one of the best second basemen in the league.

At least she didn't act like the squealy, giggly girls at school. He sighed. And she didn't call him up all the time like some of the girls did. That's when Shayna and Shari would really tease him.

"Ooooh, Brett," Shari would yell, holding out the phone. "It's your girlfriend, Jessica! Woooo wooo!"

Then Shayna would make loud kissing sounds against her hand. Then they'd both laugh loudly.

Sisters. What a pain! he thought.

Brett dialed Marty's number and went outside again. There was no way he wanted his sisters to hear him. And he especially didn't want them to know he'd called a girl—even if it was just Marty.

"What?" squeaked Marty after she heard Brett's plan. "Are you crazy? We'll never get the bases back that way. You'll get suspended. Plus, the rest of us might get in trouble too," she finished.

Brett frowned. "But Marty," he said, "we have to teach those jerks a lesson." He paced back and forth outside the back door. Why didn't she understand?

"How are we gonna teach those guys a lesson by getting in trouble?" Marty asked. "I'm with Dwight. Let's just whip 'em on Saturday. That'll teach 'em a lesson.

"And besides," Marty continued. "I have another idea about the bases."

"Oh yeah?" Brett asked. He stopped his pacing.

Marty usually did have pretty good ideas.

"Let's spy on the Pirates tomorrow. They're practicing at the other field. We can ride over on our bikes. It's not too far. We'll hide behind the equipment shed. That way we can listen to what they're saying. There are lots of bushes around that shed, remember? They'll never see us," Marty said.

"Why do we need to listen to what they say? Do you think they'll talk about taking our bases?" Brett asked. He kicked the toe of his shoe against the house.

"*Those* losers? You don't think they wouldn't blab about how smart they were to steal our bases? Are you kidding?" Marty asked.

Brett could almost see Marty grinning as she talked. "Yeah, you're right," he said. "Randell has such a big mouth. He even bragged to his little sister."

"And Bill and Norris are *so* obnoxious," Marty said. "During homeroom, they're always bragging about something. Actually," she said, "I'm kind of surprised they haven't said anything. Maybe they're finally getting smart," she joked. "Naaaah!"

"Right!" Brett snorted. "Not in *this* lifetime." He looked down at the side of the house. Whew, his shoe hadn't left any marks. His parents would ground him for sure.

"Anyway, we have to know where the bases are. Then we can plan some really good revenge," Marty said.

"Well, I've got homework to do," Marty sighed. "I

didn't do my rough draft right last night. I have to do it over again for English. See ya," she said.

Brett hung up the phone. Marty's idea might work. It should give them the answer they needed about the stolen bases. Of course, he already knew the answer. He'd call José and Dwight and tell them the new plan.

****

The next morning, the bell rang for snack. Brett hurried to his locker. He was supposed to meet Dwight there and explain the plan. Dwight had been busy doing homework when Brett called the second time. Brett couldn't understand how Dwight could spend so much time on homework.

Marty would be waiting too. Ryan and José said they'd come also. They might need to make some last minute plans about spying. Brett raced around the corner to his locker.

Thud!

"Unnh!" Brett gasped, almost falling backward.

"Hey, watch where you're going, moron!" a voice rudely exclaimed.

Brett looked up. It was Bill from the Pirates. Right next to him, Norris and Randell were grinning wickedly.

"Having some kind of a problem, creep?" Bill sneered. He rocked back on his heels. Norris and Randell kept grinning. Their thumbs were hooked in their belt loops.

"No, but *you'll* be having a problem pretty soon, idiot," Brett snapped back.

"Oh yeah? Wanna start something?" Norris asked. He unhooked his thumbs from his jeans and began flexing his fingers. He took a step toward Brett.

Brett looked around quickly to make sure no teacher was looking. This was perfect. He could just punch these guys out right now and skip all the spying stuff.

"Yeah, maybe," Brett said. He couldn't wait to slug Norris right in the middle of his ugly face. He took a deep breath.

"Hey, what's going on?" Dwight suddenly appeared behind the three Pirates.

Dwight was pretty sure he knew what was going on. Brett was just about to get himself into a lot of trouble again. Dwight frowned. Good thing he showed up when he did.

José, Marty, and Ryan were right behind Dwight. The three Pirates turned to look at Dwight and the others.

"Take a guess about what's happening," Brett said sarcastically. "The zoo just let out."

Brett knew he'd missed his chance. Why did Dwight always have to interfere?

"Jerk-face here ran right into me," complained Bill. He shoved his hands in his pockets.

"Jerk-face? You mean Norris?" Marty asked. "Your own teammate ran into you? No wonder you guys can't score during a game. You even run into each other in the halls at school!" she said.

She knew she'd probably said too much. But it felt good. She hid a smile.

Bill's face darkened. He took his hands out of his pockets. "Pretty smart mouth for a girl," he muttered. "You just wait..."

"Time to clear the halls. Everyone outside for snack break," warned a teacher's voice.

Mrs. Chen suddenly appeared around the corner. "Let's go, guys," she said. She stood and waited.

Norris and Randell began shuffling down the hall. Bill glared at Brett. Then he followed his friends.

"Must be feeding time at the zoo," Marty whispered to her teammates. They headed down the hall too. But they kept their distance from Norris, Randell, and the others. The five Dodgers followed the path under the trees.

"You almost got yourself suspended again! Don't you know that?" Dwight accused Brett. He shook his head in disgust. What was he going to do with Brett?

"Yeah, Old Lady Chen was lurking right around the corner," Marty said. She imitated Mrs. Chen's walk. The others laughed.

Then Dwight stopped. "You've gotta watch what you say too," Dwight cautioned Marty. She made a face.

Dwight went on. "I keep telling you, just beat 'em in the game. Mouthing off will just get you in trouble. My uncle always says, 'Don't get mad, just get even.' " Dwight jumped up and touched a branch that was hanging down.

"Yeah, yeah," Marty sighed. She scuffed her tennis shoes on the dirt.

"So, what is this plan about spying on the Pirates at their practice?" Dwight asked. He turned around to face them, walking backward.

"Okay," Marty said enthusiastically. She loved plotting tricks and stuff. It was her favorite thing to do. "We'll meet at the bike racks right after school. We have to beat the Pirates out of the building.

"Then we'll ride really fast down to Blaisdell Park," Marty continued. "We can leave our bikes in the bushes around the corner. That way those losers won't see them. Then we'll run for the bushes next to the equipment shed. They'll never see us." She stopped. "How's that for a plan?" she asked, looking at the circle of faces around her.

"What if they catch you?" Dwight asked. He reached for a leaf and tore it into little pieces.

"Aaaah, they won't. They're too stupid," José joked. He kicked an acorn out of the way. It smacked up against the tree trunk.

"If they do, so what?" Brett asked. "We can be at the park if we want to, right?" He shoved his hands into his pockets.

"Yeah," echoed Ryan. "It's a free country, isn't it?" He copied Brett, putting his hands into his pockets too.

"You know what?" José said. "I just thought of

something." He looked serious. "Mr. Wagner lives down the block from me."

"So? Why do we care where the Pirates' coach lives?" asked Marty. She looked at José.

"I was just thinking that I should check him out," José answered.

"You don't think he took the bases, do you?" Marty asked.

"Mr. Wagner?" Brett almost sputtered. "He'd do anything if he thought it would help his team. Think of how he coaches them to play dirty in a game. The umpires think he's a jerk."

"Like you never slid into a base with *your* cleats up? And Coach Espinoza *never* gets mad at an umpire over a call?" teased Marty. "I don't think so!"

She gave Brett a little shove and shook her finger at him. "Ah-ah-ah!" she said grinning.

"Listen," José interrupted. "I'll try to be around when Mr. Wagner comes home from practice. He always parks on the street. When he opens his trunk to get out equipment, I'll just happen to be standing there. I can check his trunk for the bases." José bent down and picked up another acorn. He snapped it between his fingers. It flew through the air. "I'll get him!" He grinned.

"Good idea," Marty agreed. "In the meantime, just be out at the bike racks as soon as you can after school. We have some spying to do, team."

4

Spying on the Pirates

"Shhhhh!" Marty whispered. She squinted through the leaves. Her nose tickled. She felt like she was going to sneeze.

Next to her, Brett rustled leaves as he moved to the right. He was having trouble seeing.

"You shhhhh," he replied angrily. He pushed a twig out of his face. He was already tired of spying. And the

Pirates' practice was only half over. Why did everyone think they needed proof? He knew who had the bases. And he could make his own plans for revenge.

"Look. They're heading in for batting practice," José's voice was soft. "Maybe now we can finally hear them say something about the bases." He sighed and squirmed uncomfortably.

Marty felt her face flush. After all, it had been *her* idea to spy on the Pirates. But so far, the Pirates hadn't said anything about bases. Well, that was okay. They weren't sure the Pirates had taken the bases anyway.

It seemed as if they had been hiding here for hours. Leaves were prickling her. Twigs were poking her. Her muscles ached from crouching low. How did Brett play catcher squatting down like this all the time?

"Here they come," Ryan whispered excitedly. He peered through the branches.

"It's about time," Brett said sarcastically. He leaned forward too.

The Dodgers watched tensely. The Pirates hustled in from the outfield where they had been warming up and practicing their fielding. Their voices carried across the field.

There was talk about school, little brothers, homework, teachers—but nothing about bases. The Dodgers were getting impatient.

Then Bill, Norris, and Randell walked up to the equipment shed. They were getting their own bases for infield practice. They were so close. Marty was sure they could hear her breathing.

"Good thing *we* have bases to practice with," Norris called to Randell and Bill who were inside the equipment shed. Norris tossed a ball high in the air. It landed neatly in his glove.

Randell grinned as he walked out. "Uh-huh," he agreed. He and Bill brought their bases out of the equipment shed.

Brett scowled. That sounded pretty suspicious. He looked over at Marty. She raised her eyebrows at him.

"Too bad for the wimpy Dodgers. No bases for practice," Bill added. He gave Norris a wide grin. "Gee, I sure hope that doesn't hurt their game on Saturday," he drawled. "We're gonna fix 'em good."

"Nothing could hurt their game," Randell said. "It's so bad already. What a bunch of turkeys. Gobble-gobble!" he said, jerking his head up and down. The three boys laughed as they walked off to place the bases.

Brett fumed. His head pounded. He wanted to jump up and nail all three of them. He wanted to pound them into the ground.

"Makes you mad, doesn't it?" José whispered softly. He shook his head.

"Just cool it, Brett," Marty warned. Too bad Dwight wasn't here. He could always get Brett calmed down. She could just see Brett jumping out of the bushes. He'd push and shove the three Pirates. Then the whole team would pile on him. The three of them would have to run out and help. It would be a brawl.

"All right, sliding practice," Coach Wagner called. He was frowning.

Some Pirates took positions near the bases. Other kids lined up next to home plate.

The four Dodgers were in a perfect position to see and hear everything. And no one knew they were there.

"Okay, go!" Coach yelled. The first runner took off for first.

"Stand up, stand up!" Coach yelled. "You don't slide into first base, you numbskull. Who do you think you are? Pete Rose?" He put his hands on his hips and jutted out his chin.

Marty was happy that Coach Espinoza never called them names. Even when he got mad at them for doing something stupid.

"Round first and slide into second," Coach Wagner called to the next runner.

The kid raced to first base. He stepped quickly on the inside corner of the base with his cleats. Then he ran to second base. He slid into the base. The kid looked proud. He stood up, brushing off his pants.

"What was that?" Coach Wagner asked sarcastically. "A tea party invitation?" The rest of the team laughed nervously. "When I say slide, I mean *slide*. Where were your cleats?"

The boy looked down at his feet.

"Not on your feet, stupid. When you slid into second, where were your cleats?" Coach walked toward the player threateningly.

The boy looked uncomfortable. He stared at the dirt.

"They are *supposed* to be up. That's how you keep from getting tagged. You gotta nail the second baseman with your cleats," Coach Wagner roared.

Coach shook his head in disgust. "Where did you learn to play baseball?" he asked. He turned his back on the boy and walked away.

José and Marty looked at each other. They knew what it was like to get nailed with cleats. Ryan knew better than anyone. And he had the brace to prove it.

Geez, thought Marty. She couldn't believe a coach would actually teach players to play dirty. Now she was sure that Coach Wagner must have let the Pirates take the bases. He would try anything, just as Brett had pointed out.

"I can't wait till Saturday, Norris." Brett heard Bill's voice. Bill was waiting in line to run the bases.

"Yeah," Norris said, keeping his eyes on the guy who was running. "Me too."

"We are going to scuff those Dodgers. I'm tired of losing to a team with a girl on it," Bill said disgustedly. He kicked at the dirt with his cleat.

Marty tightened her mouth. *You* just wait, you jerk, she promised silently.

"They think they're going to beat us again. No way," Norris agreed. Thump! Thump! He socked his fist into his open hand.

"I'd like to have seen their ugly faces when they couldn't find the bases," Bill snickered. He spit into the dirt.

"Uh-huh," Norris agreed. "I wonder what would happen if they couldn't find their *gloves* next time!" He rubbed his hands together. "Course, they hardly know how to use them anyway!" He laughed.

"Hey!" Coach Wagner's voice interrupted the conversation. "This isn't a social gathering. This is ball practice," he barked. "Norris, get moving."

Brett turned to look at Marty. "Did you hear *that?*" he whispered. His face was red.

Marty's eyes widened. "I sure did," she whispered back.

José's jaw had dropped. "They took 'em. They really did! Now they're going to take our gloves too!" José's eyes narrowed. "My glove," he whispered. "I can't play without my own glove." He rubbed his palms together.

The four watched the rest of the drill in silence. Marty glanced at Brett. He looked furious. She worried about what he might do. He was already rubbing his hand over his fist. If only Dwight were here. He would know what to say to Brett. In fact, Dwight would probably know what to do about this whole thing.

"Where do you think the bases are?" Ryan whispered to José.

José shifted his weight uncomfortably. "I don't know. But I'll check out Coach Wagner's trunk this afternoon.

He might have them in there." He frowned.

"That's the type of thing Coach Wagner would pull," Brett agreed quietly. He narrowed his eyes. He stared at the coach through the leaves.

"Hustle in and sit down," Coach Wagner called from the pitcher's mound. Cleats pounded the dirt. The thud-thud of gloves hitting the bench filled the air.

Panting, the boys plopped down on the bench. Some wiped their faces with the sleeves of their shirts. Others just let the sweat drip down their faces. Norris turned his baseball cap around.

"Rally time," he joked to Randell, who grinned in return. He leaned forward on the bench.

Coach Wagner stood facing his team, his back to where Marty, Ryan, Brett, and José were hiding. His feet were spread apart. His hands were on his hips.

Marty could just barely see him. She had to peer around Brett, José, and Ryan. It was hard to see the faces of the Pirates. They were in the shadow of the dugout roof.

"Shhhhh!" Brett said to the others, leaning forward to hear. Maybe Coach Wagner would confess right then and there!

"You all know what game is this Saturday," Coach Wagner began in a loud voice. "I don't want to see any of the screw-ups I saw the *last* time we played the Dodgers. No errors—*no errors*—do you hear?"

Brett saw Norris lower his head. Oh yeah. Norris had

thrown the ball to second instead of third. He had forgotten to pick off the lead runner. Brett smiled.

That error had gotten Brett into scoring position. Then Dwight had hit Brett in to score!

"I'm sick and tired of hearing this girl-on-the-team stuff too," Coach Wagner went on. "Play your own game. But for crying out loud, don't get beaten by this team again."

Marty felt her face get hot. She didn't know why some people had to make such a big deal about a girl on the team. She was one of the best second basemen in the league—girl or boy!

"And my last words to you," Coach Wagner said, "are these: No one ever won a ball game by being nice." He started to walk away, but then he stopped. He turned back to face the team. "I told you before—don't let anything get in the way of your winning. Now let's get this equipment put away."

Don't let anything get in the way of winning, Marty repeated to herself. What did he mean by that? What else would the Pirates try to do to them?

5

Locker Room Face-Off

Brett was walking with Dwight to P.E. "You should have been there. You should have heard them," Brett fumed to Dwight.

Clang! Clang! Clang! Brett's fist thumped against every other locker they passed in the hall.

"Yeah," Dwight agreed. "When you called last night, I couldn't believe it."

Dwight was just relieved that Brett hadn't done anything dumb. The whole time he was baby-sitting, he was thinking about what his friends were doing. He wished he could have gone.

Having a little brother and a mom who worked long hours got in the way. Sometimes he wished he could just hang out with his friends. Dwight sighed.

But his mom always told him, "You're the man of the house, Dwight." It wasn't so easy not having a dad.

"...so we're thinking about planning stuff to do to them during and after the game." Brett's voice interrupted Dwight's thoughts. Uh-oh, Dwight thought. He hoped he hadn't missed anything important. Dwight looked at Brett.

"Uh, sounds like a good idea," Dwight said quickly.

"Let's go," Brett said. They hurried through the double doors of the gym. "I can't afford any more tardies. I'll get detention again from old Beak-Face." He pretended to pull his nose out and make it longer.

Dwight grinned. Brett had nicknamed just about all their teachers. The names were perfect for them too. Old Beak-Face was actually Mr. Pomeroy. His nose did look as if he should be digging worms out of the ground. And then his brown hair. It stuck almost straight up in the air. With his long neck and Adam's apple, he really did look like a bird. Dwight snickered. Brett would *really* get in trouble if Mr. Pomeroy heard *that!*

Brett and Dwight made their way through the lines of

lockers and benches. Boys everywhere were changing into their P.E. clothes. Locker doors clanged shut. Voices called to each other.

"Did you steal my socks again, you geek?"

"Oh no, my mom put my *sister's* shorts in my bag!"

"Did you see that new girl in math today?"

Dwight headed off in one direction and Brett in the other. Brett rounded the corner leading to his P.E. locker and stopped. Right next to his locker—*his* locker—were Bill and Norris. Just what did they think they were doing?

He should just walk up there and punch their lights out. Then he stopped. He narrowed his eyes. They had their heads down and were whispering to each other. What were they planning?

His mitt. His catcher's mitt was in his bat bag. And his bat bag was in his locker. Were Bill and Norris planning to steal his mitt?

He clenched his hands into fists. Just let them touch his stuff. He would turn Bill and Norris into dog meat for sure.

"Hey! What are you doing by my locker?" Brett asked angrily. He doubled up his hands into fists.

"Hey. Calm down, friend," Bill drawled. He rocked back and forth on his heels. "We're just paying a social call." He and Norris exchanged grins.

"Get outta here," commanded Brett. He took a step toward them.

"What are we today? Shy?" taunted Norris. "We'll shut our eyes while you change." He put his hand over his eyes. "Ooooh!" he hooted.

Brett's face got hot. And his heart was racing. Wouldn't he just love to pop them one. He clenched his fists tighter.

But then he could almost hear Dwight's voice saying, "So, what will I do for a catcher if you get suspended for fighting?"

No, he told himself. He took a deep breath. Dwight's voice faded away. He relaxed his fists. He'd just bully them out of here.

"Close your eyes only if you can't take it," Brett sneered. "This isn't where your lockers are anyway. So get out of my face." He took a second step forward.

"Ooooh!" Bill exchanged glances with Norris. "Getting tough now, are we?" He grinned rudely.

Brett pressed his lips together tightly. He would just love to see Bill's face with a big purple shiner. Norris would look colorful with a bloody nose too. No, he reminded himself. He couldn't let his team down. He took a deep breath. Just ignore them, his dad would say.

Brett positioned himself between the two boys and his lock. He didn't want them to see his combination. He expertly twirled the dial. Click! It opened, revealing his bat bag and his gym bag.

"A bat bag!" Norris said. "Look at that! A bat bag!" he repeated. "Do you play baseball?" Norris asked in a high voice. He grinned evilly at Brett.

"Gee," Norris continued, looking at Bill, "I didn't think this guy played any *baseball*, did you, Bill?" They snickered loudly.

Just shut up, Brett wanted to shout at them. He took his gym bag out of his locker and unzipped it. If only they would just leave him alone.

"Gentlemen!" Brett heard old Beak-Face's voice. "Get to your lockers and get changed or you'll get tardies. I'll be happy to have you serve detention on my shift," he said.

Old Beak-Face's smile stopped just below his eyes. It made him look even more like a vulture. Brett hid a smile. Old Beak-Face kept walking down the aisle.

"Just wait for Saturday," Brett hissed to Bill and Norris. "We'll see who plays baseball and who doesn't." He narrowed his eyes and glared at them.

"Threat? Was that a threat?" Norris asked. He looked at Bill in mock surprise.

"I don't know how anybody who plays with a *girl* can threaten anybody!" Bill said triumphantly. He pranced around the bench on tiptoes. He took his arm back, pretending to throw a ball. Then he released it, flicking his wrist forward limply.

That did it. Brett wheeled around, preparing to shove Bill hard against the lockers.

"Hey!" Dwight's voice rang out behind Brett. He stopped and relaxed his shoulders. Saved again, he thought. His forehead felt a little sweaty. He had almost started a fight right here in the locker room. Old Beak-Face would have had plenty to say about *that.*

Now that Dwight was here, Bill and Norris would leave for sure. No one wanted to mess with Dwight, who was one of the biggest guys in the grade.

Norris and Bill looked at each other. Without a word, they turned and left.

"What was going on?" Dwight asked. He dropped down on the bench. He began tying his shoelaces.

"They were hassling me," Brett said. "I thought I was going to have to punch them out. You came up just in time, I guess," he admitted. He felt a little light-headed.

"What were they hassling you about?" Dwight asked.

"Oh, you know. The same old things. At first, when I came up, they were hanging around my locker." Brett began tying his shoes too. "Then they wanted to know why I had a bat bag. They said they didn't know I could play baseball," Brett said. He looked disgusted.

"Those jerks!" Dwight shook his head.

Brett grinned wryly. "Yeah. And, of course, the old stuff about us playing with girls." He snapped his laces into a knot.

Dwight's face darkened. His jaw tightened. "You know," he began, "those guys are such jerks. I want to whip them on Saturday so bad!" He adjusted his sock and stamped his foot on the ground.

Brett's face grew thoughtful. "I was thinking," he

said. "Maybe we should be sure Coach Espinoza takes the equipment bag home after practice today." He looked at Dwight.

"Do you think they'd try to take that too?" Dwight asked. He reached down and fixed his other sock.

"After all the stuff they've been saying? I wouldn't be surprised at *anything* they did," Brett said. "Except if they said they're sorry. That would surprise me." He grinned. "And that'll never happen!" He stood up and waited for Dwight to finish.

Dwight knew Brett would go crazy if the Pirates took the catcher's equipment. Then he'd lose his catcher for sure. He shook his head. Was this War on the Pig-Heads going to get out of control?

6

Watch Out for Those Pirates!

Brett was impatient. He kept checking the clock. When would school be over? Finally, the bell rang.

"Let's go!" Brett shouted to Dwight. He raced down the hall toward the doors. He had to get to their ball field. None of the Pirates better be hanging around.

Coach Espinoza would open the shed as soon as he got there. Then Brett could see if his catcher's equipment was still in the bag. He had worried about it all afternoon.

Brett wished his parents could afford to buy him his own catcher's gear. He frowned. But it was too expensive.

When he got a little older, he could get a job. Then he could pay for the equipment himself. He'd keep it at home. Not in some equipment shed.

Brett unlocked his bike from the rack. He hopped on and his legs began pumping hard.

He could hear Dwight's voice behind him.

"Hey, man, wait up!"

Then José called, "Is there a fire somewhere?"

Marty and Ryan were too busy pedaling to yell anything.

Brett rode around the corner and squealed to a stop. The others rode up, panting. They all stopped.

Brett scanned the ball field across the street. "Well," he said, "I don't see anyone, do you?" He shaded his eyes with his hand.

"No," Marty answered. She grinned. "Lucky *we* don't have bushes around *our* equipment shed!" She brushed the hair out of her eyes.

"Oh, Ryan, I saw everyone else at school today," José said. "So I already told them. I didn't have a chance to tell you. I checked out Mr. Wagner's trunk yesterday." He spun the pedal of his bike with his foot. It twirled round and round.

"So were they there?" Ryan asked. "Did you see our bases in his trunk?" He tightened his grip on his handlebars.

"No," José said disappointedly. "I saw some bats and a bag of helmets. I looked really carefully too." He sat back down on his seat.

Coach Espinoza's car pulled up in the parking lot next to the practice field.

"Let's go," called Brett, already racing across the street on his bike. Now Coach could open up the equipment shed. Then he could see if the catcher's equipment was still there.

Coach was already standing by the shed. He put his bag down. He fished the keys out of his pocket. Brett dropped his bike on the ground. He ran over to the shed.

"You're in an awful hurry today, Brett," Coach said, turning to look at him. "Can't wait to practice, eh?" he joked. "Can't wait to run those bases?"

"Yeah," Brett admitted. "I want to see if the bases are back. And I just want to be sure the catcher's equipment is still there." He stood waiting impatiently.

Coach looked at him curiously. "Why wouldn't your equipment be there?" he asked. His keys jingled as he reached for the padlock.

"Well, you never know," Brett said worriedly. Hurry up, he thought as Coach stuck the key in the lock

The key turned. The padlock snapped open. Coach unhooked it from the latch.

Cr-r-r-r-eak! The metal door swung open. Brett looked in over Coach's shoulder. Where was it? He couldn't see anything for a moment. There it was! The blue equipment bag sat in a weak shaft of light from the open door. Brett made a grab for it. Quickly he unzipped the bag.

A wave of relief washed over Brett. It was there! There was all his catcher's equipment—mask, shin guards, and chest protector. But there were no bases in the shed. They were still gone.

"You kids are taking this stealing idea a little bit too far, don't you think?" asked Coach. He shook his head.

"Coach, you should hear what they've been saying," Brett said. He hauled the bag outside into the light.

"What who's been saying?" Coach asked.

"The Pirates," Brett answered. "They've been making lots of threats."

"Hey, what did you find out from the other coaches?" Marty asked, walking up to them. She put her cap on.

"Let's get everyone together in the dugout. Then I'll tell you all at once," Coach said with a smile. He picked up his clipboard and walked to the dugout.

Quickly, the rest of the team assembled on the bench.

Marty studied Coach's face. Had he found out? He was smiling. But then, he was always smiling. She couldn't tell.

Brett hoped Coach would have some answers. Of course, *he* didn't need answers.

"Okay," Coach said. "I called all the other coaches in the league. They were surprised to hear the bases were gone. Their teams all practice on this field once in a while. In the last week, though, only two other teams used the field. They were the Braves and the Pirates." He tapped a pencil on the clipboard.

Brett turned to look at Dwight. "I told you so," he whispered. He thumped his fist in his mitt.

"The coach of the Braves said they practiced here yesterday, Wednesday. So they didn't have any bases to use. The coach of the Pirates—" Brett shifted on the bench— "said they practiced Monday. But he said he clearly remembered putting the bases away." Coach looked at each player in turn.

"Yeah, right," Marty whispered to José. She slumped back on the bench. "Wagner would say anything," she added.

"He remembered because there was a problem," Coach Espinoza said. He paused.

"What was it? What was the problem, Coach?" José blurted out. He leaned forward.

"They had trouble getting the bases out of the pins in the ground. They were stuck. The straps were coming apart too. Since it was such a problem, he clearly remembers putting them in the shed," Coach said. He walked up and down in front of the bench.

"But he'd lie about it, wouldn't he, Coach?" Brett asked. He ground his fist into the pocket of his glove.

"Yeah," Marty agreed. "We know him. He'd say anything." Including cracks about girls, she snapped silently.

"Just a minute," Coach said. He frowned. "That's pretty serious. You can't accuse someone of lying with no evidence." He looked intently at the players.

"Well," Dwight said, "we know what kind of a coach he is." Dwight straightened his shoulders. He looked at his friends on the bench.

"The stuff he does to umpires," began Marty.

"And the junk he has the team do," continued José.

"He would do anything to win—*anything!*" exclaimed Brett.

"Yeah," echoed Ryan. He reached down and rubbed his ankle. Comments and grunts of agreement from the rest of the team filled the air.

Coach Espinoza grinned. "Listening to all of you, I would guess that Coach Wagner wouldn't win the Coach of the Year Award."

Coach Espinoza stopped and looked at all of them. "I don't always agree with everything Coach Wagner does. And he's not one of my best friends. But I want you to know that I don't think he lied to me about the bases." Coach tipped his cap back on his head. He rubbed his forehead.

"Well, maybe *he* just doesn't know that his team stole them then," Marty said. "Maybe he didn't lie, but they would."

Mutters of "Yeah" and "That's right" filled the air. The Dodgers shifted restlessly on the bench.

"Well, so where are our bases, Coach?" Brett demanded. He jutted out his chin. They had to be *somewhere,* didn't they? And he knew the Pirates had them.

"There has to be an explanation," Coach agreed. "I did call the rec center and talk to the secretary. She wasn't much help. She didn't know anything about any bases missing. So she asked the director. He couldn't help either. He said all the bases should be in their equipment sheds." Coach raised his eyebrows and sighed.

"There is an explanation. Seems more and more like the Pirates to me," Brett replied. The bench erupted in agreement.

"Settle down," Coach said. "I want you to concentrate on playing ball, not on the Pirates and some missing bases. And, by the way, I don't think they did it. Now let's get practicing. We've wasted too much time already."

The players hustled out to the field. They began throwing to warm up. Brett jogged out to face Dwight. He wound up for a throw.

"Just watch where you put your glove," Brett warned. "Especially when it's your turn for batting practice." He threw the ball to Dwight's outstretched glove.

"Do you really think they'd come around here?" Dwight asked.

Marty overheard Dwight's question. "Don't forget. I saw Bill and Norris hanging around the last time we practiced. I wouldn't..."

Dwight cut her off. "I think we need to get off this Pirate thing. If we don't, they'll beat us for sure. Which is more important—the bases or Saturday's game?" Dwight finished.

"Well, I don't care," Brett answered, frowning. "I've got some great plans for revenge at Saturday's game. Those losers are gonna be sorry they ever heard of us!"

7

The Twins Confess

The next morning at school, Brett rushed to his locker. Everyone would be waiting at the snack bar already. His mom had been running late, so now he was late too.

Of all the days for his mom to be behind. He had more important things to do than clean up the kitchen. Why couldn't Mom make his troublemaking sisters do it all?

Shayna and Shari had been bugging him all morning too. Frowning, he remembered what had happened at breakfast.

****

"So, big brother, how is the great detective?" Shari teased. She poured the last of Brett's favorite cereal into her own bowl.

"What do you mean 'great detective'?" Brett asked. He picked up the empty cereal box and shook it. "Hey, brat! You ate all my cereal!"

"Maybe you can find some more cereal, Brett. Just like you found your stolen bases!" Shayna joked. "You're the great detective, aren't you?" She began to giggle.

Both the twins began to laugh out loud, milk dribbling out of their mouths.

"If I ever lose anything, Brett, I'll be sure to call you!" Shari spluttered cereal all over the table as she began to choke with laughter.

"Get a life, will you," Brett said crossly. He got up to get another kind of cereal from the cupboard.

Just then his mother dashed in.

"Brett! Be nice to your sisters, would you for once, please? And clean up all this milk for me. I'm already late for work."

His mom walked over and kissed him. Then she rushed out the door. Unfair, unfair, Brett grumbled to himself. Life was just unfair.

"You guys better shape up," Brett barked. "Or I'll take care of you!"

He slammed the cupboard door and sat back down. He noticed that the twins had gotten quiet. He looked up at them. They were looking at each other strangely.

"Are you really gonna fight Randell?" Shari asked slowly. She looked over quickly at Shayna.

Brett sat still, holding the box of cereal. "What makes you think I would?" he asked.

"Well," Shari looked at Shayna, "we heard you talking on the phone with Dwight. We snuck around the house so we could hear you." She looked down at her cereal bowl.

Those little brats! He felt his face get hot. He gripped the box of cereal tightly. They had been listening to his phone calls!

"And we decided we don't want you to get suspended," Shayna said. She sighed and swirled the cereal around in the bowl with her spoon.

"Especially since when that happens, Mom and Dad get in really bad moods," Shari added. She licked her spoon.

"Brett," Shayna began nervously. She and Shari looked at each other. "We have to tell you something."

"Yeah? What? What's so important?" he asked suspiciously.

Shari took a deep breath. "We have a confession."

"Yeah," Shayna agreed. They looked at each other again.

"We made up that story about Randell's sister. We just wanted to tease you." Shari hung her head. Clink! Clink! Her spoon tapped nervously against the side of the bowl.

Brett stared. "You *what?*" he croaked.

"We're sorry, Brett," Shayna said. "We thought it would be funny at first. See, we don't like his sister. She's a brat. But then we thought about it. And we don't want you to get in trouble."

Shayna stood up. She carried her cereal bowl over to the sink. Shari quickly followed.

Brett's mouth dropped open. "You *made it up?* You made up the whole thing?"

"Uh-huh," the twins answered together. Their backs were to him. They rinsed their bowls busily in the running water.

They don't even have the guts to look at me, Brett thought angrily.

"Oh, man," Brett said. "Just think about how much trouble I almost got into—and over something that didn't even happen." He frowned. "You guys owe me, or I'm gonna tell Mom and Dad." He shoveled a spoonful of cereal in his mouth.

"You can't," Shari said turning around, "because then they'll find out you were gonna fight Randell!" She smiled proudly.

Brett clenched his fists. What could he do with these oversized brats? "Then I'll just make sure you behave yourselves. Or else you'll be sorry you ever started this," he threatened. He chomped down on another bite of cereal.

The twins looked worried. Brett thought about what he could do. Suddenly, he had a great idea.

"If I catch you spying on me or listening in on my

phone conversations, I'll tell everyone in your grade that you both like Mike Maloney."

"EEEEEEEW!" the twins shrieked together. "EEEEEW!"

"Oh, you can't. I could never go to school again," Shari said earnestly. She raised her eyebrows and opened her eyes wide.

"We'll be good, Brett, we promise," Shayna said, trying to look innocent.

"No more stories, honest," Shari promised.

"You'd better be telling the truth this time," Brett warned. He frowned at them.

****

Brett shut his locker, still thinking about his morning. He rushed down the hall and out to the quad. Everyone was already there.

"Sorry I'm late," Brett said. "Twin trouble again." He made a face.

"What are you going to do with those skyscrapers?" Dwight asked. "I know," he grinned. "I'll introduce them to my little brother, and they'll pulverize each other. There won't be anything left but a couple of hair bows and a squirt gun."

Brett laughed. "Yeah. Well, maybe after this morning, that's not a bad idea." He paused. "I gotta tell you guys something." He shifted his backpack on his shoulder.

"What?" Marty asked quickly. "What happened?"

She stepped in closer.

"My sisters told me something. Listen to this. They made up all that stuff about Randell telling his little sister that he took the bases." Brett turned his mouth down in disgust. "Can you believe that?"

"But that doesn't mean that the Pirates *didn't* take our bases," Marty reminded him. She looked at Brett.

"No, it sure doesn't," agreed José. "Especially after all that stuff we heard them say at their practice!" He shook his head. "They just about said they did it!"

"Wait a second, guys," cautioned Dwight. "The twins' story *was* one of the first things that tipped us off to the Pirates, wasn't it?" He looked at his friends' faces.

"No," Brett said. "I already figured they had done it. Remember all the junk they were saying to us after the last game?"

"That's right," Marty said. "Okay, so that story was wrong. But that doesn't change the fact that the Pirates are going to get scuffed on Saturday, right?" She grinned.

"Yeah, Brett," agreed José. "Tell us your ideas about how we're going to get revenge on those losers on Saturday." He crowded in closer and grinned.

"First," Brett began, "when you're running the bases and you stop on a base, lean down. Pretend you're tying your cleats. But pick up a handful of dirt. Then when you run and slide, throw it in the air in front of the Pirate. He won't be able to see to tag you!" Brett grinned.

Brett reached down and grabbed an imaginary fistful

of dirt. Then he flung it into the air. He and Marty gave each other a high five.

"That sounds kinda like bad sportsmanship," cautioned Dwight. "Aren't there better things we can do?"

"I don't know," Marty said grinning. "Sounds like fun to me!" She copied Brett, reaching down and grabbing some pretend dirt. Then she pretended to throw it in Dwight's face. He jumped and blinked. Then he grinned at her.

"Yeah, fine, as long as no one does it to *you* when you're playing second," Dwight said.

Marty paused. Dwight was right. "Yeah, I guess so," she admitted slowly.

"What else?" asked José.

"Well, we can slide in with our cleats up. Just like they do," Brett argued.

Marty looked doubtful. "I'm not too sure I like *that* idea," she said. "I know what it feels like. Ryan *really* knows what it feels like. Plus, the Pirates would probably be even worse if they *knew* we were trying it too."

Brett sighed in exasperation. "Well, then, run into them when you're running the bases. And when you're covering a base and have to make a tag, be sure to block the bag down low so they can't knock you over." He crouched down and shoved an imaginary base runner.

"That's fine. That'll work," agreed Marty. She brushed her hair out of her eyes.

"Yeah, I don't have a problem with that," Dwight

said. He looked at the others.

"I really want to get those jerks," Marty said. She ground her fist into her open hand.

"Yeah, I'm tired of all the junk they're saying and doing too," agreed Dwight. "We just have to be careful."

"Not wimpy, though," argued Brett.

Dwight grinned slowly at his friend. "Yeah, okay, not wimpy, Brett," he agreed.

"We'll get 'em tomorrow in the game," Brett promised. "We'll get 'em *good!*"

8

The Pig-Heads Mouth Off

It was Saturday morning. The whole Dodger team was sitting in the dugout at Blaisdell Park. They were waiting for Coach Espinoza to look up from his clipboard.

"I wish we were playing on our regular field," Marty whispered to José. "Are you ready to whip them?" She looked around at her teammates on the bench beside her.

"Yeah. Are you?" José asked. "I can't wait to smash those jerks." He leaned forward and smacked his fist into his glove.

"All right, team," Coach Espinoza began. "Before we go out and warm up, I want to say a couple of things." Coach looked over at the other dugout.

The Pirates were already there, rustling through their bat bags. They were calling and hooting to each other. It was easy to hear most of what they were saying.

"*This* is gonna be an easy game," Norris bragged. He flung his hair back out of his eyes and jammed his cap on his head.

"Like playing my grandma," Bill added, unzipping his bat bag.

"Naaah," Norris said. He laughed. "Like playing your *great*-grandma!" The others laughed.

"What do you expect from a team with a *girl* on it?" Randell sneered. He made his voice screech way up high when he said "girl."

Out of the corner of his eye, Brett could see Marty scowl. Brett was glad she had heard them. When she was mad, Marty really hit the ball. Then they'd beat the Pig-Heads for sure.

"All right," Coach continued. "I know there have been a lot of problems between you and the Pirates." He looked hard at Brett. "Some of you have almost gotten into fights." Coach shook his head. "That doesn't help anyone, especially the team."

Brett looked down at the dirt under his cleats. Great, he thought. Just what he needed—another lecture about his temper. He sighed.

WHO STOLE THE BASES?

"I want you to put this stolen base stuff out of your heads during the game. Let's play heads-up baseball. You deserve to beat this team. You will if you concentrate on what you're doing. Don't think about all that other stuff. That's what causes problems. So," Coach paused and looked at each player in turn, "I expect each of you to do your best out there today. Now let's warm up. Let's show the Pirates how it's done," he finished with a grin. He made a "thumbs-up" gesture with his free hand.

"Coach!" A sharp, yet deep voice made Brett jump. He looked up.

Coach Wagner of the Pirates was standing right in front of their dugout! Even through the chain-link fence, his eyes looked cold and mean.

"Yes?" Coach Espinoza wheeled around to face him.

"I have to tell you and your team something," Coach Wagner said. He rubbed his chin.

This is it! Marty thought excitedly. He was going to admit stealing the bases! He was going to apologize! She elbowed Brett. He grinned at her. Next to her, José looked at her and mouthed the word "Yes!"

"Harrumph!" Coach Wagner cleared his throat.

Did he look nervous? Hah! Marty thought. It's tough to admit you're wrong, isn't it?

"I just want you all to know something," Coach Wagner began. He frowned.

Brett fought to hide his grin. Here comes True Confessions! He almost laughed out loud.

"I'm going to be watching your team pretty closely today." Coach Wagner stared at each of them. "Last time you tried to bat out of order."

What? Brett couldn't believe his ears. He turned to look at Marty. Her mouth had dropped open. Next to her José blinked his eyes. Down the row of kids, Brett could see Dwight shaking his head.

"Don't think you can pull anything like that again," Coach Wagner growled. "We play a fair game. We'll be watching to see that you do too." He glared at the Dodgers.

"Thank you for the warning," Coach Espinoza said dryly. Coach Wagner turned on his heel. He walked back to the Pirates. For a moment, the Dodgers sat in stunned silence. Then they all began talking at once.

"They *stink!*" Brett said furiously. He spit into the dirt.

"No kidding!" Marty agreed.

"Let's whip them good," Dwight said. He thumped his fist in his glove.

"Listen up," Coach Espinoza said. "We're not going to lose this game because we're too mad to concentrate. They think we'll be too mad to play well. But we'll show them what we're made of! Now let's get going."

Brett strapped on his shin guards. As he walked toward home plate, he put his catcher's mask on. Dwight was on the mound ready to warm up.

Marty grabbed her glove and hustled out to second base. Everyone else jogged to their places. The infield began throwing the ball in drill order.

Dwight warmed up with Brett. Thunk! The ball landed perfectly in Brett's catcher's mitt. He threw it back and gave Dwight the sign for a breaking ball.

Brett worked hard to frame the pitch for Dwight with his mitt. He knew he had to give Dwight a perfect target. Thunk! He did it! That was Dwight's best pitch. He knew they would kill the Pig-Heads with it today.

The Dodgers ran off the field and into their dugout. "Hey," Brett said to Dwight. He took off his catcher's mask and plopped down on the bench.

"Yeah?" Dwight asked.

"Pitch your breaking ball low and inside today. Those Pig-Heads really had trouble with that pitch last game. Remember?" Brett said grinning.

"You bet," Dwight answered. He smiled. "I remember. Randell even accused me of trying a brush-back pitch to hit him!" He poured himself a cup of water from the jug.

"Uh-huh! Coach Wagner even tried to get you pulled from the game!" Brett laughed. "At least the umps know how Wagner works. They don't pay much attention to him.

"But of course," Brett added, "if you should happen to hit a Pirate with a wild pitch —by accident of course— I won't complain!" He gave Dwight a fake punch on the arm. Dwight grinned at him.

"What are you guys laughing about?" José asked. He drank thirstily from a cup of water.

"You know," Dwight said, "just some pitching strategy. And about how closely I can pitch one inside!"

He stuck his cup in the chain-link fence enclosing the dugout. He wound his arm in a big circle to loosen it.

"Oh yeah," José said, his eyes sparkling with mischief. "It's great when they have to jump out of the way!" He jumped back from an imaginary pitch.

"There's no way *they're* going to own the plate when *I'm* pitching," Dwight said. He straightened his shoulders. He sat down on the bench and looked at the infield.

They watched as the Pirates took the field for their warm-up. "Check out Randell," Marty said. She pulled her baseball cap down low on her forehead. "Thinks he's cool, doesn't he?" Randell flipped the ball expertly in the air while he waited for his catcher to warm him up.

"What a geek," Dwight said in disgust. About that time, Randell dropped the ball. He bent down quickly to get it off the ground. The Dodger bench snickered.

"He's coordinated too," José said. He laughed.

Bill, at catch, rotated to face the Dodger dugout. He glared. "Just shut up!"

"Ooooh! Vicious!" Marty said loudly.

Brett and Dwight snickered loudly. The rest of the Dodgers laughed.

"What a bunch of losers," José said.

"All right, team," cautioned Coach Espinoza. He was standing by the fence working on the batting order. "Let's not make trouble. Leave the personalities out of it." He shook his head at them.

"But how can we leave the personalities out of it?"

Brett whispered angrily to Marty. "They are such jerks. They stole our bases and everything."

"Don't let the stolen bases and all that other junk get to you," Dwight reminded him. "Let's just play our game and beat 'em again." He watched Randell wind up on the mound.

"But what about our bases?" Marty asked. "Aren't we going to make them give them back to us?" She turned to look at Brett and waited for his answer.

"We'll figure something out," vowed Brett. He scowled. "We'll just pile on them after the game. We'll rub their noses in the dirt. Then they'll tell us where the bases are." He looked at his fingers and flexed them. "These babies are going to get a work out!"

Dwight turned away from watching the pitching. He looked at Brett and sighed. "Come on, man! Lighten up. That's not the way to do it. I keep telling you over and over. What are you, brain dead?" He grinned to take the edge off his words.

"We'll start by scuffing them in the game," Dwight continued. "Let's keep them from scoring. No runs for the Pirates. And remember, run hard right into them. Too bad if they're in the way on the bag!" Dwight twirled a ball in his hand. "We'll kill 'em today. I just know it."

Marty watched the Pirates throw the ball around the bases. They looked really up today. Her stomach tied itself in a little knot. What if the Dodgers *didn't* win today?

9

The Big Game Begins

Marty could feel her heart beating fast. She stared at the batter from her spot near second base. It was hard to see his eyes under his helmet. It was Bill, though. He was their lead-off batter.

Please strike him out, Dwight, she thought. Last game, she was sure Bill had tried to cleat her when he slid into second. At least she would be ready for it this time.

But just wait until she got a run. She'd come sliding into the bases with her cleats up too, if that was the game they were going to play.

"Wimps play with girls!" Her cheeks burned as she remembered what the Pirates had yelled. Well, she'd show them how *wimpy* she was. She thumped her fist into her glove. She crouched down in ready position.

Dwight wound up and pitched. Thunk! Right into Brett's mitt.

"Steee-rike one!" The umpire motioned with his arm.

Bill turned around and stared in disbelief at the umpire. "That was way outside!" he protested.

"I'm making the calls here," warned the umpire. "Let's play ball."

Brett grinned as he stood up to throw the ball back to Dwight. This was a good sign. First pitch—first strike. They were going to do it. He just knew it. They had to win this game!

"Steee-rike two!" The umpire yelled his call.

"Just a minute here!" Brett heard Coach Wagner's voice from the first base line. He was standing there ready to coach his runners. *If* they ever got on, Brett snickered to himself.

"I could see from here. That was high. What is your strike zone today?" he questioned the umpire. "Whatever you feel like?" He put his hands on his hips and frowned.

"Coach," warned the umpire, "leave the calls to me. If you want to make a protest, then I'll ask the field umpire."

"Yes, I do," barked Coach Wagner. He turned and glared at the field umpire.

Marty watched the drama unfold from where she

stood between first and second.

Behind her, she heard the field umpire yell, "It was a strike—*sir!*"

Marty grinned. Sir! she thought. It sounded as if the umpires weren't going to let Coach Wagner get away with anything today. She looked triumphantly over at Danny covering first. He grinned back at her.

The half inning finished quickly. Three up and three down.

Dwight wiped the sweat from his forehead as he took a seat in the dugout. That was quick. He always felt better after he had one inning behind him. All those hours of practice in the side yard next to his apartment building were paying off.

"José! Let's go!" Coach Espinoza called. José was their lead-off batter. He already had his helmet and batting gloves on. He hustled out to the warm-up circle and swung the bat a few times.

Marty waited just inside the dugout with her bat in her hands. She was batting second.

Danny grabbed a third helmet off the ground. "Where're my batting gloves?" he asked worriedly. Danny looked at the gloves in the fence.

"Your gloves are missing?" Dwight asked, frowning.

"Check your bat bag," Marty suggested, peering around the pole.

Danny looked under the bench. He unzipped his bag.

Dwight thought about his pitching. He was on today.

Wouldn't he love a no-hitter. Especially against the Pirates. If only he could pitch well enough to throw brush-back pitches. He'd love to send the Pirates home with some bruises. He frowned, watching Danny rifle through his bag.

"Here they are," Danny said in relief. "I guess I never took 'em out of the bag."

Whew, Dwight thought. He was glad the gloves weren't missing. Brett would have blamed the Pirates for sure. Who knew what he might have done. Dwight didn't want to get into a brawl.

Brett looked over at Dwight. "Were you thinking what I was thinking?" he asked.

"Yeah," Dwight said. "I'm glad he found them." He tipped his cap back and wiped his forehead again.

"Well," Brett admitted, "in a way, I kind of hoped he wouldn't." A wide grin stretched across his face. "It would give me another reason to pound their faces into the dirt!"

Dwight shook his head, grinning. "You've gotta do something about that attitude," he joked.

"Just wait till I get up," Brett promised. "By then, we'll have runners on. I'll send it over the fence!" He swung an imaginary bat.

Brett checked to see where his teammates had put their gloves. Everything was safely under the bench inside the dugout. No one had flung a glove anywhere that a Pirate could pick it up.

When there was a lot of excitement during a game, no one noticed what was happening *off* the field. Today,

Brett decided he'd be sure to watch. Especially after the batting glove problem. He knew José would watch too.

"Maybe we shouldn't hang our batting gloves on the fence," Brett suggested to Dwight. "Too easy for someone walking by to snag one."

"Maybe," Dwight agreed. "But if we're sitting right here..."

"You never know!" Brett said. He turned to look at the cluster of batting gloves on the chain-link fence behind them. "If they can steal the bases..."

"Any missing batting gloves," Brett continued, "and you'll see what will happen to the Pirates! I'd love to grab one red-handed!" He grinned evilly. He looked up to see José ready for the first pitch.

"Steee-rike one!" The umpire's call caused the Dodger bench to take notice.

Brett was surprised. What was wrong with José? He usually went for the first pitch. That's what Coach always said to do. He had just watched it go by.

Brett saw a huge grin on Bill's face behind his catcher's mask. Bill stood up and threw the ball back to Randell on the mound.

José shook his head in disgust.

"You'll get it, José," Marty called encouragingly.

"Make it your pitch, José," Dwight yelled.

"Make him pitch to you," Brett hollered.

Thwack! José hit a line drive between shortstop and second. It got past the center fielder.

José was off and running. He rounded first. Then he raced for second. The center fielder had the ball. He winged it to the second baseman.

Thud! Marty could even hear the sound from where she was standing in the warm-up circle. The second baseman and José collided on the base.

"Safe!" yelled the field umpire, sawing the air with his arms.

José got up, brushing the dirt from his baseball pants. He was grinning. The second baseman was leaning over, trying to walk off the collision. Marty looked over at Dwight with a grin.

"He ran right into him, didn't he?" she said.

"Yup!" Dwight said, giving her a high five.

Marty took a deep breath. She walked up to the plate.

"A girl?" jeered Bill from behind his catcher's mask. "*Girls* don't play baseball. Oh yeah," he added. "That's right. I forgot. You *don't* play baseball."

Marty could feel her anger build. Their rude comments just made her want to beat them even more.

She turned to watch Coach's signals. He gave her the bunt sign. Good call. She could advance José. With luck, she *might* make it to first. She was pretty fast.

The pitch hurtled toward her. Slap! She bunted the ball just to the left of the first base line. She raced for first. She saw the overthrow sail over first's head. She made it!

"Score! Score!"

"Go hard! Go hard!"

The team and fans were yelling at José. From her safe position, she saw José slide into home. He knocked Bill flat. Marty grinned. Take that, you jerk, she thought.

Danny hit Marty home with a triple. Then Brett got a double, sending Danny home in a cloud of dust.

The Pirates were yelling stuff at the Dodgers. "Swing!" they'd yell.

"Out! He was out!"

"Girlie team! Girlie team!"

The fans were going crazy. They yelled from the stands. Everyone felt the tension and the strong rivalry. The War on the Pig-Heads was on!

Then Dwight hit into a double play. When left field caught Ernesto's fly, the inning ended. At the end of the first inning, the score was Pirates 0, Dodgers 3.

The jeers and bad sportsmanship from the Pirates continued throughout the game. When the Pirates were at bat, they rattled the dugout fence when Dwight was winding up for a pitch. They hooted and howled at strikes. They yelled the same stuff over and over.

"Strike? Whaddaya mean, strike?"

"Girls don't play baseball! Hey, guys, we're playing girls' baseball!"

Coach Wagner ignored what his team was saying. He looked as if he didn't even hear them. Marty figured he'd probably told them everything to say.

As expected, some of the Pirates slid into bases with their cleats up. Luckily, the Dodgers knew what to watch for. So no one was getting hurt.

Then when the Dodgers were at bat, the Pirates were even worse.

"Swing!" they'd yell at any pitch.

"Awwww, ump!" they'd holler at the umpire after a ball was called. "Looked good to me!"

"Wimp!" someone would call if the batter didn't swing at a pitch. "Loser!"

And of course there was the constant "Hey, batter-batter-batter-batter!" Of course, the Dodgers did that too. Somehow it sounded much worse when the Pirates did it, though. The yelling made the Dodgers even more determined to win.

During their at bats, Marty and others shared stories on the bench.

"When I slid into third, you should have heard what he said to me!" Ernesto said.

"Did you see Bill throw down his catcher's mask? He was so mad!" Brett said, grinning.

"Norris is a jerk! When I made it to first, he had his foot on the bag and tried to trip me!" Dwight said angrily.

The Pirates got two runs in the fourth inning. Ernesto missed a fly ball and two Pirates ran for home.

"Safe!" the umpire yelled twice.

Brett felt his muscles tense. They couldn't lose this game. They just couldn't. He looked around at his teammates. Marty was frowning. Ernesto was socking his glove. José rolled his glove fingers back and forth. Even

Dwight fiddled nervously with the baseball.

The Dodgers held them for another inning. But the Dodgers didn't score, either. Brett almost slammed his bat down in frustration.

Suddenly, at the top of the sixth inning, with the Pirates up, Norris hit a double. Bill raced for home. Kevin in center field missed the cutoff throw. Brett crouched ready at home plate. But the throw never came.

Bill slid in triumphantly. Dirt blanketed Brett.

Bill got up and brushed himself off, grinning. "Tough," he sneered.

He'd like to punch that meathead. Brett looked over at Dwight. Dwight shook his head. 3 to 3. How could this happen? They had led the whole game. They had to win.

The Dodgers frowned. The Pirates hooted and howled. The fans went wild.

"Tie score! Get one more!" the Pirate fans yelled.

We're in trouble now, Marty thought.

Finally, the third Pirate got out. The bottom of the sixth and the Dodgers were finally up. The score was still tied.

José hit a fly ball. The Pirate shortstop backpedaled and trapped it neatly in his glove. Then Danny struck out. The Pirate infield gathered at the mound. They all gave Randell high fives and laughed.

Marty was up with two outs. Her mouth felt dry. She had to do it! She slammed the first pitch! It was a double.

She slid into second base in a cloud of dust. The second baseman just glared at her. Marty grinned as she stood up, brushed off, and tucked her batting glove into her back pocket.

Marty watched Brett walk up to the plate. He jammed the batting helmet down farther on his head.

Brett had to hit the ball and bring her in. She had to score. Please, let us win, she begged silently.

If Brett got out, it would still be a tie game. They'd go to extra innings. Then it would be anybody's ball game again.

Come on, Brett, she whispered silently. You have to do it! Win the game for us, please!

"Look who's up!" yelled one of the Pirates. "Hey, any luck finding your stolen bases, little guy? Maybe you and your *girlfriend* on the team could find 'em together!"

He made some loud kissing noises against his hand. All the other Pirates began to laugh and hoot.

Even from second base, Marty could see Brett's angry expression under his batting helmet. She hoped he could stay focused, even though he was angry. Brett was a good hitter. And right now, that's just what the Dodgers needed.

"Swing, wimp!" a voice behind her hooted.

Brett swung hard.

He missed. He banged his bat down on the plate in frustration.

Marty clapped her hands nervously. "Let's go, Brett. Bring me in!" she called.

10
Revenge on the Pig-Heads

Brett gritted his teeth. Get off my back, you jerks! he thought angrily. He swung the bat a couple of times to loosen up. All around him, he could hear people and kids yelling.

"Aaaah, you can't hit the ball!"

"Go, Brett! Go get 'em!" There was his dad's voice.

He could hear his mom too. "Slam it, Brett!" her voice called loudly.

WHO STOLE THE BASES?

"Come on, kid! Win the game!"

"Come on, wimp!"

"Hey, Brett! Hit a home run!" Shayna's and Shari's voices joined together in a screech.

He couldn't believe he had just swung and *missed*. The pitch had looked like a regular fastball. Too late, he had seen its spiraling drop. He had missed by a mile! His face burned. How humiliating!

Then he heard Norris' voice from first base. "Look at that. He even swings like a girl!"

That did it! He'd wipe the field with that guy after the game.

From behind him in the warm-up circle, he heard Dwight's voice. "Come on, man! You can do it! Just stay in there! Don't let 'em get to you!"

Brett's muscles tightened. He stopped. He had to stay calm.

Okay, okay. He couldn't let this get to him. The team was counting on him. He had to hit Marty in. They had to win. They had to beat the Pirates!

He took his stance and waited for the pitch. Through narrowed eyes, he saw Randell wind up.

Then—Thwack! Brett's bat connected with the ball! A solid hit—a line drive past the shortstop!

His heart beating wildly, Brett raced for first, then second as Marty slid into home!

"Safe! That's the ball game," called the umpire.

Dust rose around home plate. Marty jumped to her

feet, grinning.

They had won! And he had brought in the winning run!

The Dodgers raced out of the dugout and piled on Brett. He felt kids slapping his batting helmet, slapping his back, shaking his shoulders.

"Yeah, Brett!"

"You did it, man!"

"We beat those jerks!"

Marty slapped him on the back. "Way to go, buddy!" she crowed. "Thanks for the hit!"

"Hey, man, nice hit," Dwight said, giving him a high five. He smiled broadly at Brett.

Brett pulled off the batting helmet. He wiped his forehead with his shirtsleeve.

"All right, team. Line up," called Coach Espinoza. He was grinning too.

Brett, Ryan, Marty, José, and Dwight joined their teammates in a line. The Dodgers were shoving and pushing each other and laughing.

But the Pirates' line was quiet. A few Pirates were muttering stuff. Some of them had their heads down. They weren't even looking at the Dodgers. Others, like Norris and Randell, looked as if they were getting ready to say something really nasty.

Marty stopped. She stared at some of the Pirates at the end of their line. "Hey," she whispered to José. "Look what they're doing! *Again!*" She frowned.

"What?" José asked. He looked at the Pirates lining up.

"Some of them are spitting on their hands and rubbing them in the dirt! Sick!" she exclaimed. She rubbed her hand on her baseball pants.

José wrinkled his nose and spit into the dirt next to his cleats. "That's pretty sick, all right," he agreed. Then he grinned. "Of course, we could do it too!"

"Yuck!" Marty said loudly. She made a face.

Behind her, she could hear Brett's voice. "I'm gonna get that Norris and rub his ugly face in the dirt."

"Come on, man..." Dwight began. He turned around to face Brett.

"Well, we beat 'em, all right?" Brett argued. "But do we have our missing bases yet? Just let 'em say one thing—*one thing* about those bases, or anything—and I'm gonna make sure they..." Brett took a couple of steps out of the line toward the Pirates.

"Just wait, all right?" Dwight interrupted. He grabbed Brett by the arm and steered him back into line. "Wait until we have a chance to plan something. You don't need to go off and get yourself in trouble."

"Yeah, yeah," Brett muttered. "Okay, keeper," he joked. He tried a small smile.

The players' cleats shuffled in the dirt as the two lines passed each other. They slapped hands and mumbled halfheartedly, "Good game."

"Good game, good game, good game," Marty said. She tried to keep her eyes on the guys she'd seen spitting all over their hands. But she couldn't tell which ones they

84

were. Sick, she thought.

As Marty slapped hands, she tried to move quickly. She didn't want any sick Pirate slobber on *her* hand.

Ouch! Someone had just hit her hand really hard and jammed a cleat down on her foot! She fought tears. No way. There's no crying in baseball, she reminded herself, quoting a line from one of her favorite movies. She bit her lip to keep the tears back. She jammed her cap down on her head.

Well, let those dirty Pirates do what they wanted. The Dodgers had won. Nothing else mattered much anymore.

"Good game," Coach Espinoza said with a wide smile. "Grab your bags and let's go to the outfield. Everyone help pick up the equipment, please."

Brett stuffed the catcher's equipment into the equipment bag and zipped it shut. Then he helped Dwight and José drop the batting helmets onto the pole they carried them on. Marty helped Ryan collect the balls. Kevin and Ernesto picked up the water jug and the extra cups. Everyone else picked up bat bags and stray cups that had fallen on the ground.

Marty dropped down on the grass next to Dwight. She began untying her cleats. She looked at Coach. Suddenly, she thought about the bases. She had forgotten about them. So where were they?

"Everyone's here," Coach Espinoza said happily. "Well, didn't I say that if you kept your concentration, you could beat them? I'm really proud of..."

WHO STOLE THE BASES?

"Excuse me, Coach?" A man in a blue park uniform stood next to Coach Espinoza.

Coach looked as if he didn't like the interruption. Dwight wondered if maybe Coach was just about to tell them he knew where the bases were. Maybe Coach Wagner had suddenly "remembered" where he had left them.

"Yes?" Coach asked, patiently.

"I'm Bob Weems from the parks and recreation department. I've been trying to get you on the phone for days." Mr. Weems shifted nervously from foot to foot.

The man looks worried, Dwight thought. Dwight shook some dirt out of one shoe.

"Yes, and...?" Coach said patiently.

"Your bases are finally repaired. You probably noticed that the straps have been coming loose. I have them with me in the truck. I'll take them back to the other field for you. Unless you want to take them back with you now. You're going back to the practice field with the rest of your equipment, aren't you?" The man looked hopefully at Coach.

Everyone stopped moving. Marty's hands froze in midair. Dwight stopped with one cleat half off. Brett's jaw dropped. José choked on the water he was drinking from his jug. Coach Espinoza just stood there blinking at the man.

"You knew the bases were missing, didn't you?" asked Mr. Weems. He looked puzzled. "You must have noticed when you had practice. I'm sorry it took so long. I thought we could get them back to you in a couple of days. I took them to be repaired myself."

He looked a little embarrassed. "I—ah—guess I forgot to tell anyone in the office about it. I only just today heard that you had called. I'm afraid I'm not very organized," he apologized. His shoulders slumped a little as he finished.

Coach Espinoza began to laugh. "That's okay! No problem," he spluttered.

All the Dodgers began to laugh and groan. Brett socked his forehead. Dwight just shook his head. Marty and José looked at each other in disbelief.

Mr. Weems looked even more puzzled. "I don't get the joke," he said. "Is there some joke?" he repeated.

"Whoa," Dwight whispered to Ryan. "He doesn't know the *half* of it!"

"No," exclaimed Brett. "Just that we thought another team stole the bases from us. We're kinda in this little war with them. We were sure they had done it. They're such dirt bags anyway." He grinned as he shook his head.

"Yeah," Marty said. "And we have been trying to get back at the Pirates this whole week!"

Mr. Weems began to smile. "Well, at least you know the story now," he said.

"So, team, how about telling the Pirates you found your bases? You can tell them you're sorry you suspected them," added Coach Espinoza. "Don't you think they should know?" He grinned widely at everyone.

Brett looked at Marty. Marty looked at Dwight. José looked at Ryan. Everyone on the Dodgers began to snicker.

"No way!" yelled Brett.

"Not in this lifetime!" Marty said.

"Yeah, right!" José said. He elbowed Ryan, who grinned.

"When donkeys fly!" Dwight exclaimed. "We'll never tell them anything!"

What a great day, Brett thought. The Dodgers had beaten the Pirates. And now they had their bases back. The Pirates would never find out where the bases had been. No one on the Dodgers would ever tell them!

And just wait till their next game! Brett grinned. He already knew the Dodgers would scuff the Pirates again. They would destroy them, for sure.

In the meantime, he, Dwight, Ryan, Marty, and José would make sure the Pirates *knew* they would be losers again too. He could hardly wait!